CKL

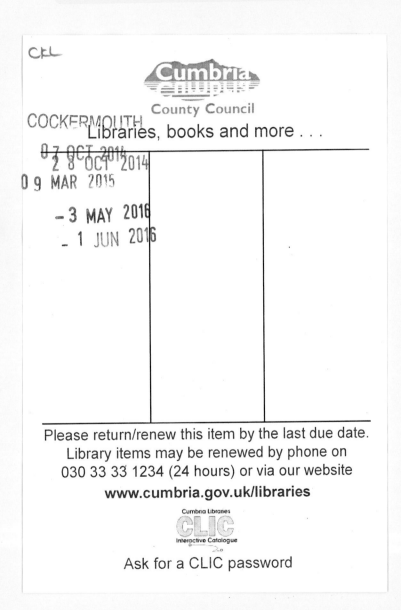

Cumbria
County Council

COCKERMOUTH

Libraries, books and more . . .

07 OCT 2014
2 8 OCT 2014
0 9 MAR 2015

- 3 MAY 2016
- 1 JUN 2016

Please return/renew this item by the last due date.
Library items may be renewed by phone on
030 33 33 1234 (24 hours) or via our website
www.cumbria.gov.uk/libraries

Cumbria Libraries
CLIC
Interactive Catalogue

Ask for a CLIC password

What Can I Make Today?

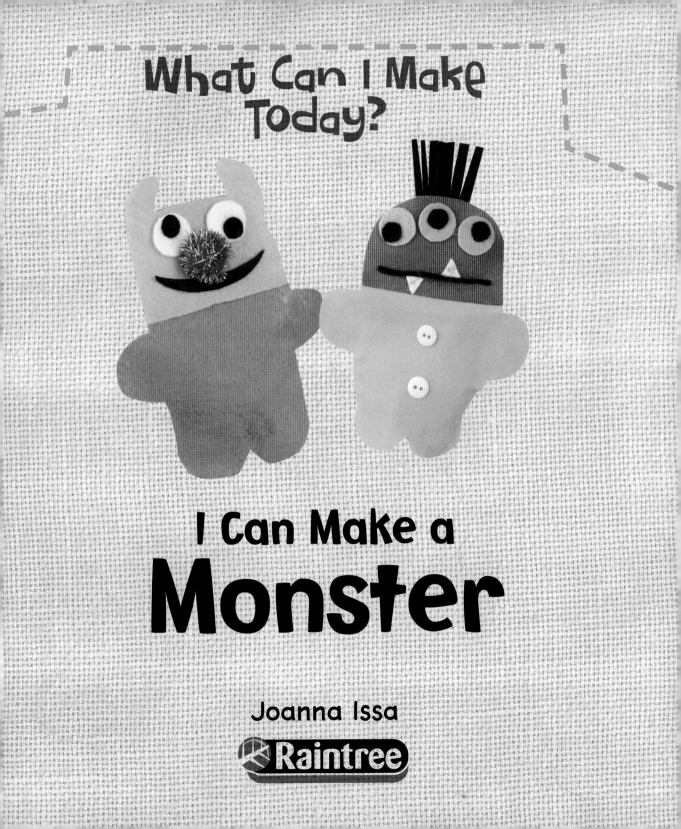

I Can Make a
Monster

Joanna Issa

Raintree

Raintree is an imprint of Capstone Global Library Limited, a company incorporated in England and Wales having its registered office at 7 Pilgrim Street, London, EC4V 6LB – Registered company number: 6695582

Edited by Penny West
Designed by Philippa Jenkins
Picture research by Elizabeth Alexander
Originated by Capstone Global Library Ltd
Production by Victoria Fitzgerald
Printed and bound in China

ISBN 978 1 406 28402 7
18 17 16 15 14
10 9 8 7 6 5 4 3 2 1

British Library Cataloguing in Publication Data
A full catalogue record for this book is available from the British Library.

Acknowledgements
We would like to thank Capstone Publishers/ © Karon Dubke for permission to reproduce photographs.

Cover photograph reproduced with permission of Capstone Publishers/ © Karon Dubke.

We would like to thank Joanna Malivoire for her invaluable help in the preparation of this book.

Every effort has been made to contact copyright holders of material reproduced in this book. Any omissions will be rectified in subsequent printings if notice is given to the publishers.

Disclaimer
All the Internet addresses (URLs) given in this book were valid at the time of going to press. However, due to the dynamic nature of the Internet, some addresses may have changed, or sites may have changed or ceased to exist since publication. While the author and Publishers regret any inconvenience this may cause readers, no responsibility for any such changes can be accepted by either the author or the Publishers.

Contents

What do I need to make
    a monster puppet? 4

Make the body 6

Make the head 8

Make the eyes 10

Make the mouth 12

Decorate the monster 13

Make a different monster 16

What can you make today? 20

Monster templates 21

Picture glossary 23

Find out more 24

Some words are shown in bold,
like this. You can find them in
the glossary on page 23.

What do I need to make a monster puppet?

To make the body and the head of the monster, you will need **felt**, the body and head **templates**, a pen and scissors.

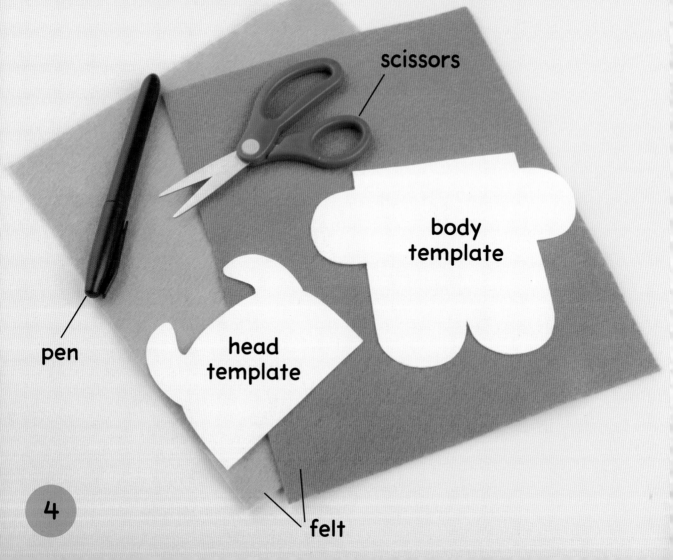

scissors

body template

pen

head template

felt

To make the templates, photocopy pages 2l and 22, and then cut out the shapes.

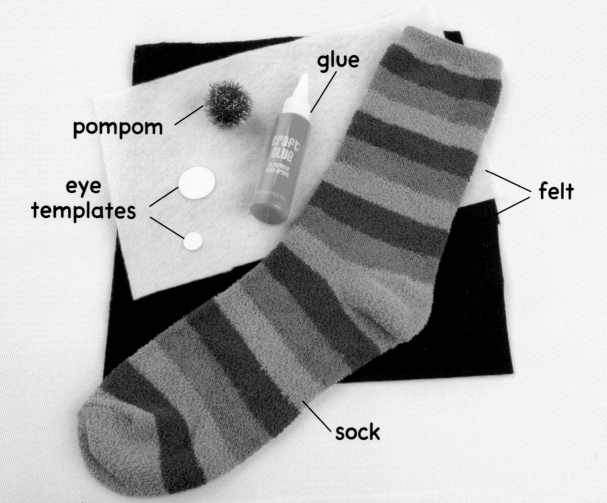

glue

pompom

eye templates

felt

sock

To decorate the monster, you will need the eye templates, yellow felt, black felt, glue, a **pompom** and a child's sock.

Make the body

Place the body **template** on the **felt** and then draw around the shape.

Cut out the body.

Make the head

Place the head **template** on the **felt** and then draw around the shape.

Cut out the head.

Make the eyes

Place the large eye **template** on the yellow **felt**. Draw around it to make an eye, then cut it out. Do this again, so you have two large circles.

Place the small eye template on the black felt. Draw around it to make the middle of the eye, then cut it out. Do this again, so you have two small circles.

Make the mouth

Cut a thin strip of black **felt** for the mouth.

Decorate the monster

Put all the monster body parts on a table. Glue the head onto the body, then glue the eyes and the mouth onto the head.

Use a **pompom** for the nose.

Push card inside the sock to stop the sides sticking together. Glue the monster onto the sock, then let the glue dry. Remove the card.

Now your monster is ready to play with.

Make a different monster

You can make different monsters. Use the **template** on page 21 to make a different head. Give your monster three eyes.

You can give your new monster **fangs**.
Cut small triangles from white **felt**,
then glue them onto the mouth.

Give your new monster hair. Cut a rectangle shape from **felt**, then make small strips in it to look like hair.

You can add buttons to your
new monster.

What can you make today?

You could make a cute or a creepy monster for a puppet show or a Halloween party.

Monster templates

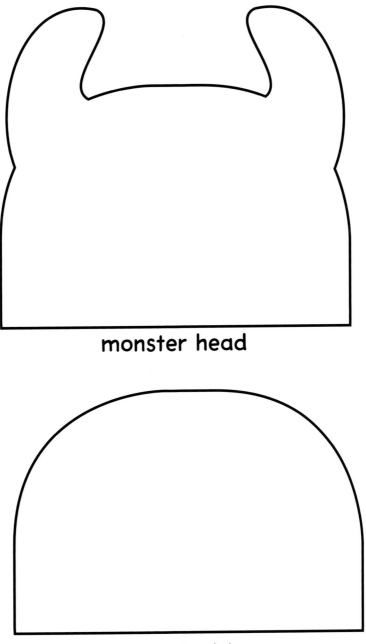

monster head

monster head without ears

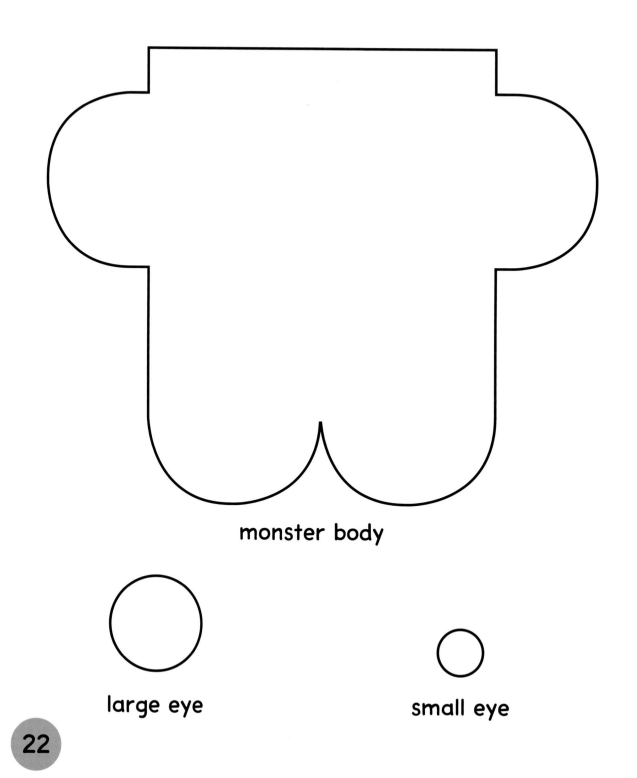

monster body

large eye

small eye

Picture glossary

fangs long pointed teeth

felt type of fabric made from wool

pompom round ball made from wool

template pattern of a shape cut out of paper

Find out more

Books

Crafty Creatures, Jane Bull (Dorling Kindersley, 2013)

Fun with Fabric (Clever Crafts), Annalees Lim (Windmill Books, 2013)

Making Puppets (Make Your Own Art), Sally Henry and Trevor Cook (Franklin Watts, 2011)

Websites

www.bbc.co.uk/cbeebies/makes
On this website, you can read about and make art projects.

www.museumofchildhood.org.uk/learning/things-to-do
This website has fun make and do activities for children of all ages.

Index

body 4, 6-7, 22
decorate 5, 13-14, 19
fangs 17, 23

hair 18
nose 14
templates 4, 5, 21-22, 23

24